CW01052129

NEBS
MANAGEMENT
DEVELOPMENT

SUPER S E R I E S

THIRD EDITION
Managing Resources

Controlling
Costs

Published for
NEBS Management *by*

Pergamon
Open
Learning

Pergamon Open Learning
An imprint of Butterworth-Heinemann
Linacre House, Jordan Hill, Oxford OX2 8DP
225 Wildwood Avenue, Woburn, MA 01801-2041
A division of Reed Educational and Professional Publishing Ltd

A member of the Reed Elsevier plc group

OXFORD   BOSTON   JOHANNESBURG
MELBOURNE   NEW DELHI   SINGAPORE

First published 1986
Second edition 1991
Third edition 1997
Reprinted 1998

British Library Cataloguing in Publication Data
A catalogue record for this book is available from the British Library

ISBN 0 7506 3307 7

The views expressed in this work are those
of the authors and do not necessarily reflect
those of the National Examining Board for
Supervision and Management or of the publisher.

NEBS Management Project Manager: Diana Thomas
Author: Raymond Taylor
Editor: Ian Bloor
Series Editor: Diana Thomas
Based on previous material by: Peter Elliot
Composition by Genesis Typesetting, Rochester, Kent
Printed and bound in Great Britain

Contents

Reflect and review   65

Workbook introduction

1 NEBS Management Super Series 3 study links

Here are the workbook titles in each module which link with *Controlling Costs*, should you wish to extend your study to other Super Series workbooks. There is a brief description of each workbook in the User Guide.

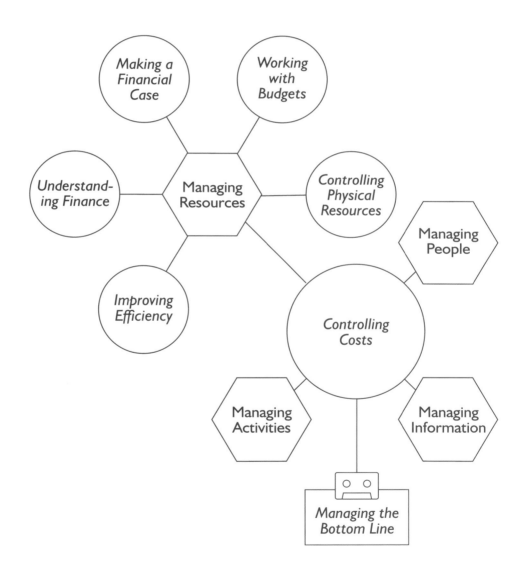

2 S/NVQ links

This workbook relates to the following elements:

B1.1   Make recommendations for the use of resources
B1.2   Contribute to the control of resources

It will also help you develop the following Personal Competences:

- focus on results;
- influencing others.

3 Workbook objectives

In our daily lives we all need to control expenditure (another name for costs), so that we have money to spend and save. Companies also need to control costs to help them make a profit and reinvest for the future. Business organizations must be competitive to survive so keeping costs under control is an essential activity. Other organizations need to control costs to make the best use of resources.

We need to distinguish between cost control and cost reduction. Cost reduction is usually undertaken as a systematic programme to reduce existing levels of costs, perhaps because a company is facing difficulties, or needs to be able to match the prices of competitors. It may involve changing working methods, new sources of supply, or employing fewer people.

Cost control is a continuous and routine management function. It is almost certainly part of your job, for costs aren't just the concern of accountants and senior managers. What's more, you and your workteam contribute to the final cost of whatever goods or services you provide, so it is important that you take an active interest in cost control.

In this workbook we will look at ways of controlling and monitoring costs. You will improve your understanding of these matters so that you and your workteam can be more effective.

Throughout the workbook we look at examples from different organizations. Some may or may not be directly relevant to you at the moment but the principles may be appropriate to something you do at work. Costing techniques were developed for practical purposes. You should use them when relevant and not when they would be too costly to use or of little benefit. Of course, this means that you must be aware of what is available to you. Remember the value of a breadth of knowledge even where something does not immediately appear relevant to you.

3.1 Objectives

When you have completed this workbook you will be better able to:

- understand the types of costs and the way standard costs are determined;
- identify the main areas of cost;
- understand how to arrive at target costs for control;
- describe cost centres and the allocation of costs;
- maintain cost consciousness.

4 Activity planner

The following activities need some planning and you may want to look at them now.

Activity 11   Here you are being asked to think about obtaining 'value for money' from your workteam and you may like to think about this as you study your workbook before reaching that activity.

Activity 14   Here you are being asked to think about breakdowns in production or delivery of service and ways in which you could counteract these problems.

Activity 36   You are invited to consider how to communicate the need for cost consciousness to your workteam.

Some or all of these activities may provide the basis of evidence for your S/NVQ portfolio. All Portfolio Activities and the Work-based assignment (on page 63) are sign-posted with this icon:

Portfolio of evidence

This icon will always show the elements to which the activity or Work-based assignment relates.

Note that the Work-based assignment suggests that you speak to your manager, finance director or to your colleagues in the accounts office about the way in which costs are controlled in your organization.

You might like to start thinking now about who to approach and arrange to speak with them.

Session A Costs

1 Introduction

At home if your expenses or costs are high in comparison to your income, your life can be difficult. Say, for example, that the electricity, gas and telephone bills are all due at the same time and your wages are only enough to pay two of them. What do you do?

Let's assume you negotiate time to pay but realize that the same problem is likely to occur next quarter. You'll have to decide whether to turn down the heating, switch off the lights or cut back on phone calls.

Businesses can find themselves in similar situations. It is up to you and everyone in your organization to be concerned about the costs of whatever you produce or supply, just as you should be concerned about quality.

Business organizations in the private sector who do not control costs may go out of business. Organizations in the public sector with high and increasing costs will need to make severe cuts in their activities and will attract a great deal of criticism from the public and government of the day. As a first line manager, you'll need to be concerned with costs and their control.

In this session we will look at the different kinds of costs and how you can help to control them.

2 Organizational costs

The **total costs** of an organization are made up of such things as:

- wages and salaries;
- electricity, gas and other utilities;
- purchase of steel, wood, stationery, X-ray plates or whatever raw materials the organization uses;
- payments for services from transport to cleaning.

These costs are deducted from the **sales** of the organization; the difference is **profit**. Profit might also be called operating surplus by organizations in the public and voluntary sectors.

Sales (or income) − Costs = Profit (or operating surplus)

1

Several ways of setting prices are based on the idea of determining costs and then adding a percentage for profit. Identifying costs is, therefore, important:

The implication of this is that an organization can either **increase its prices** or **decrease its costs** to become more profitable or to alter the level of its operating surplus.

But, there are dangers with these courses of action.

Activity 1

3 mins

Suppose the price of your favourite biscuits was suddenly doubled.

Jot down **three** things you might do.

_____

_____

_____

EXTENSION 1
You can explore the relationship of costs and pricing further in Chapter 5 of David Irwin's book *Financial Control for Non-Financial Managers.*

Well you might:

■ buy fewer biscuits;
■ stop buying the biscuits;
■ buy biscuits made by a competitor;
■ buy an alternative product, such as cake;
■ cut back on something else so you could afford the biscuits.

People who buy your organization's products may choose one of these options if you increase your prices. You probably don't have much to do with fixing selling prices, but you **are** in a position to affect costs. By reducing these you can help your organization and that's what we'll concentrate on.

As a first line manager you will be concerned with the following costs:

■ labour costs, which also include national insurance and pension contributions;
■ materials costs, which can include a wide variety of things from bandages to bar steel;
■ overheads.

3 Direct and indirect labour costs

Wages which can be totally allocated to a particular product are usually called **direct labour costs**. Some examples of direct labour are:

- painting a product;
- welding a part;
- sewing a garment;
- dealing with customers;
- processing data;
- a hairdresser doing a cut and blow dry.

Wages which cannot be allocated to a particular product are **indirect labour costs**. Examples of indirect labour arise from:

- maintenance costs;
- cleaning;
- employing a sales force;
- operating a marketing department.

None of these can be allocated directly to a particular item of production, even though they are essential for an organization as a whole.

In the following time sheet I have filled in the columns which show the type of work completed and the hours taken.

	Time sheet						
Name		No.			Week ending		
Dept	Work completed	Material used		Start time	Finish time	Total hours
		Qty	Description			
Mon	Operating production machines					8
Tue	Cleaning					8
Wed	Operating production machines					8
Thu	Operating production machines					8
Fri	Maintenance					8
Sat						Nil
Sun						Nil
Signed		Total hours: 40 Checked			(Supervisor)	

It shows that:

■ 24 hours were spent operating a production machine. These are **direct labour hours** as they can be allocated to the product made;

■ 8 hours were spent cleaning and a further 8 hours were spent on maintenance. These are **indirect labour hours** as they cannot be allocated directly to products.

Direct labour costs will increase or decrease in proportion to the production activity being carried out and for this reason are called **variable costs**.

Indirect labour costs happen all the time, whether something is being produced or not. They are **fixed costs**.

We will look at the significance of fixed and variable costs a little later on.

The above illustration is of work in a factory environment. However, time sheets are also used in other areas such as plumbing, mending televisions, aspects of the care sector and so on.

To enable management to plan ahead with confidence, it is very important that time sheets or other systems for monitoring staff workloads are completed carefully and correctly to enable direct labour hours to be separated from indirect labour hours.

Let's look at an organization making two types of product, boots and shoes.

Ten machine operators work 40 hours per week, and are paid £5 per hour.

These are the only direct labour costs.

Activity 2

Write in the total direct labour cost per week.

_____

The direct labour cost per week is: $10 \times 40 \times £5 = £2000$.

In addition to this, there are other weekly costs, such as:

■ indirect labour costs;
■ purchase of leather;
■ electricity;
■ office staff salaries;
■ motor vehicle running costs.

4

In, say, a residential care home, those who deal directly with the residents would have their labour costs categorized as direct labour. Wages of cleaning staff, laundry costs, outside entertaining and so on would make up other indirect costs.

Let's say that indirect costs come to another £5000 per week in our boot and shoe manufacturing business. Weekly sales are:

- boots £6000;
- shoes £6000.

Activity 3

How much profit is the organization making per week?

Calculate this by completing the following:

Sales £_____ – Costs £_____ = Profit £_____

The total sales are £12,000 and the total costs are £7000 (£2000 + £5000), so the profit is £5000 for the week. Management can work out from this that the percentage profit on sales is profit divided by sales multiplied by 100.

$$\frac{£5000}{£12,000} \times 100 = 41.67 \text{ per cent.}$$

This figure would then be interpreted, comparing it against previous results, targets and the results of competitors to see if it is satisfactory.

In the case of a charity or other non-profit making organization where the goal is to generate surplus funds to reinvest in helping people, the calculation would be Income – Costs = Surplus.

4 Materials costs

In manufacturing, materials costs (which these days often mean component costs) can often account for more than half of the total costs of production.

In industries such as aero engineering, computer and car manufacturing, you can readily appreciate that the costs of materials such as steel, plastic and electronic equipment, will probably make up much of the total costs of the finished product. Conversely a telephone banking operation may find that materials costs account for less than one tenth of total costs.

If you work in a service industry, think about how the following could be used when dealing with stationery, ingredients for meals and so on.

4.1 Direct and indirect materials costs

We already know that labour costs can be broken down into direct and indirect categories. Materials costs can also be divided into:

- direct materials costs;
- indirect materials costs.

Direct materials costs are the costs of materials used in the products, such as:

- wood;
- steel;
- paper;
- component parts;
- ingredients for meals;
- plant food and compost.

Direct materials costs can be allocated directly and in total to an item being produced.

Indirect materials costs are the costs of such materials as:

- cleaning products;
- paper and stationery;
- lubricants.

Indirect materials costs cannot be allocated directly and in total to an item being produced.

If a material is used for different jobs, it may not be possible to allocate all the costs as either direct or indirect. Let's look at an example.

Suppose you work for an organization which makes a range of timber products. One of the items is garden sheds, which are all painted. The same paint is used to decorate the factory premises.

Activity 4

Complete the statements below with a suitable word or words.

- The paint used on the factory is _____ _____ materials cost.
- The paint used on the garden sheds is _____ _____ materials cost.

6

The paint used on the factory premises is AN INDIRECT materials cost, because it cannot be allocated in total or directly to the making of sheds.

The paint used on the garden sheds is A DIRECT materials cost, because it can be allocated in total and directly to the making of sheds.

4.2 Stock costs

Let's now turn to the cost of materials in stock, which can be called **stock costs**. Stock costs money to buy, but there are also many costs involved in holding stock. Some of them are:

- tying up money which could be doing something else, such as earning interest;
- paying interest, if the money to buy the stock is borrowed;
- refrigeration costs, relevant to food in supermarkets;
- heating costs, if stocks (such as tropical plants) have to be kept warm;
- rent and rates on the storage space – which may be large if stocks are bulky.

Activity 5

3 mins

Just in time (JIT) techniques are used in some businesses to reduce stock holding costs. The idea is that stock is ordered to be available exactly when it is needed. Suppliers must be of high quality and very reliable for this technique to work effectively.

Peter works at a fishing port for an organization which packs fresh fish and one item he uses all the time is ice, which is purchased from an ice manufacturer.

Write down **two** costs which his organization would have to pay as a result of **buying** and **keeping** a stock of ice.

_____

_____

As well as the cost of ice his organization may have to pay:

- refrigeration costs;
- interest charges if the ice is bought with borrowed money;
- reorder costs, such as the clerical costs of preparing purchase orders and goods received notes;
- rent and rates on the building where the ice is stored;
- stock-out costs – what it would cost in lost sales and ruined fish if the ice ran out.

To help keep stock holding costs under control, management may set a **maximum stock level** for all items of stock held. This enables a calculation to be made of the maximum stock holding costs at any one time.

Let's look at another example.

Activity 6

Sahid is a first line manager for an organization which assembles hi-fi equipment. He has ten people in his workteam, and they are supposed to draw from the stores sufficient parts for only one day's work. Any unused parts are to be returned to the stores at the end of each working day.

Only one parts requisition form is completed each day for all ten team members.

For several months, the number of parts withdrawn from stores was about the same each day, with a few unused parts being returned each evening.

Sahid now notices that the number of parts drawn from stores has started to vary from day to day, and no parts are being returned at the end of the working day. However, the number of hi-fis being assembled has not changed.

On investigation, he finds that some of his workteam are building up 'private stocks' of parts. This is to save them the trouble of obtaining new parts from stores every morning and, by not returning unused parts at night, they are able to leave earlier.

Will building up private stocks of parts cause stock holding costs to increase or decrease? Briefly explain your answer.

_____

_____

_____

_____

If the workteam builds up private stocks of parts, stock holding costs will be greater than planned. The reason is that as 'official' stock levels fall, they will be reordered sooner than necessary. As a general rule, you would want to ensure that the only place stocks are held is in the stores. You may notice this problem if you work in an office. Some people may build up unnecessarily high 'stocks' of pens, paper clips, rubber bands and compliments slips.

Let's examine the costs of reordering.

4.3 Reorder costs

Costs of reordering stocks for stores may be made up of a series of costly activities, including:

- filling in purchase requests, and sending them to the buying office;
- sending out requests for quotations to possible suppliers;
- preparing purchase orders to send to suppliers, with copies going to a number of different departments in the company for recording and costing;
- receiving the goods, checking them, and preparing records to notify the purchasing office and the accounts department;
- dealing with invoices from the suppliers;
- payment by cheque or other means, and recording the transaction.

Since several different departments have to be involved, clerical costs of reordering items of stock will be quite considerable. But if stocks are not ordered in time, the organization will run out.

4.4 Stock-out costs

Just as too much stock can cause additional costs, so can too little stock. These are called stock-out costs and arise when replacement stock has not been received in time. This can be damaging.

Stock-outs can occur if:

- stock levels have fallen too low before reordering;
- suppliers take too long delivering;
- clerical errors occur with reordering;
- events happen outside the control of the company, such as strikes, or suppliers going out of business.

Imagine an advertising organization running out of letterheads. As corporate image is so important to such an organization, this could damage business.

Activity 7

2 mins

Identify **two** possible consequences of stock-out problems for a restaurant and the costs that arise as a result.

_____

_____

Some damaging things that might happen are:

- it may not be possible to provide meals and deliver a good service;
- labour is being paid for doing nothing;
- customers may buy from competitors – losing those and future customers;
- the restaurant may be forced out of business.

First line managers may be able to make contingency plans so that production can still continue if stock-outs occur. A good workteam is flexible, and we can find ways of adapting to changes and problems.

5 Overheads

Costs incurred, not easily identified with any particular process or product are called **overheads**. Indirect materials are overheads. Safety clothing and cleaning materials are examples. Other overheads include:

- insurance of stocks of materials and finished goods, machinery and people
- heating and lighting;
- rates;
- wages of people not directly involved in production or directly providing a service such as:

  - security staff;
  - maintenance fitters;
  - managers and supervisors;
  - secretaries and reception staff.

Activity 8

Which of the following are direct and which indirect material or labour costs?

	Direct	Indirect
1. Materials used to make a particular product or provide a service.	☐	☐
2. Wages of workteams whose time is spent entirely on manufacturing, or service provision.	☐	☐
3. Receptionist's salary.	☐	☐

Materials used in these ways are DIRECT materials costs, and the wages of workteams whose time is spent entirely on manufacturing or service provision are DIRECT labour costs. The receptionist's salary is an indirect cost or overhead.

Now let's complete our examination of cost headings with other types of overhead.

■ Selling and distribution overheads.

These include general overheads such as heating and lighting, and commission to sales staff, delivery costs, advertising and catalogues, maintenance of cars and lorries, expenses of sales staff, and so on.

■ Administration overheads.

These include accounting and financial costs, the hire of and depreciation of computers, office supplies and stationery, maintenance and depreciation of the building and its contents.

Retail organizations are in the business of buying and selling – **trading** in other words. Insurance companies, chartered accountants and surveyors, do not sell goods in any form. They sell a service which doesn't involve any processing of materials or selling of goods. Let's look at cost headings in such organizations.

Activity 9

3 mins

Cross out the costs below which you would **not** find in a retailing organization.

■ Components.

■ Direct labour.

■ Factory overheads.

■ Selling and distribution overheads.

■ Administration overheads.

■ Stock costs.

You should have crossed out components, direct labour and factory overheads which would be replaced by purchases costs in retailing.

Let's look now at another way of looking at costs.

6 Fixed and variable costs

You will remember that we have already said that costs which vary with output are called **variable costs**. Costs which don't are called **fixed costs**.

Let's look at an example of each.

- Variable cost

A baker sells bread and cakes in paper bags or boxes. The packaging material is directly related to the output of bread and cakes and is a **variable** cost.

- Fixed cost

The monthly repayments of a mortgage on the baker's shop is not be affected in any way by how much is sold, so this is a **fixed** cost. That doesn't necessarily mean that fixed costs don't change. Mortgage repayments can change, but the reasons for the change are not related to output.

EXTENSION 2
Sometimes fixed costs can be converted to variable costs. Take a look at Chapter 3, Action themes, in John Gittus' book *Controlling Costs* which illustrates how this works.

Often, production wages are variable as they vary with output. If a hospital increases the number of patients treated, more nurses may have to be taken on or extra overtime paid. Variable costs need not vary **exactly** in proportion to output or service provision. If a sudden drop in demand occurs, it's unlikely that people would immediately be laid off.

Now that you've examined some costs and the possibility of breaking them down into separate headings which may, or may not, vary with the level of activity in the workplace, we're ready to start examining ways in which we can control costs.

7 The first line manager's role in controlling costs

It's sometimes difficult to decide which costs are fixed and which variable. In the longer term, virtually nothing is fixed. We usually regard business rates, for example, as a fixed cost as it is a payment demanded by the local authority, and outside the control of the business. But rates vary between one town and another, and may increase or decrease from year to year. A business can, of course, reduce its rates bill. It can move!

Fixed costs are fixed over a period of time and that timescale is linked to the scale of decision making which takes place in the organization. For instance, a power generator has to make very long-term plans. It is not easy to move a power station! But the situation for an employment agency is far more fluid. On a day-to-day level, the important distinction we have to make is between the costs we can control and those we cannot.

Activity 10

Large airlines use a 'hub and spoke' model to spread high fixed servicing costs over many aircraft. All flights go to a hub airport where there are flights to hundreds of possible final destinations.

Tick the costs below which you think you can influence.

- Quarterly electricity cost. ☐

- Rent of the firm's premises. ☐

- Rental cost of each telephone line. ☐

- Quarterly cost of telephone calls. ☐

The cost of electricity and telephone calls made can be kept down by your efforts.

Perhaps you feel, particularly if you work for a large organization, that the amount of electricity you use or how many telephone calls you make doesn't make any real difference on the overall total.

To some extent you're right. If you turn off lights when you go out of a room or make your telephone call outside the peak period or through a cheaper telephone company, it will make a difference of only a few pounds a quarter.

But by setting an example to your workteam you can encourage your team members to control costs. You will also exert quite a bit of influence on other people who come into your work area, if they see that you take cost control seriously.

As a general rule, variable costs are more likely to be within your control than fixed costs, and it is these which you can most easily help keep down by your own efforts.

But what can we do about other costs which are not directly within the control of the people involved?

Let's take an example of your workteam's time. Probably how much they are paid and their pay scale would be outside your control. But you can make sure that value for money is obtained for that cost.

Activity 11

4
mins

This Activity may provide the basis of evidence for your S/NVQ portfolio. If you are intending to take this course of action, it might be better to write your answers on separate sheets of paper.

Jot down **one** way in which you can ensure that you get 'value for money' for the cost of your workteam's time. Make a note of ways in which you can implement your suggestion.

_____

_____

_____

Perhaps you said something like 'keep them working' or 'make efficient use of their time' or even 'manage them properly'. You may have started to think in detail about selecting the right people for the job and training them properly. Perhaps you could draw up a time schedule for yourself and your team.

Now look at this example.

Activity 12

2
mins

Shari's workteam uses computer terminals which are linked to a large computer at head office. Frequently they spend long, frustrating periods in front of the screen waiting for responses from the heavily loaded computer. Response time is slow and seems to be getting worse. She is able to use her workteam's time on other jobs so that their time isn't wasted so much, but the real problem doesn't go away. What can she do?

Write down one suggestion.

_____

_____

She could try a number of possibilities, for example:

- ring head office and try to find out what the problem is;
- talk to her manager about it and get him or her to take it up.

If Shari was to report 'a general feeling' that response time is getting worse, it may not meet with much reaction. It would be more helpful if she kept a record of the problems and noted exactly what was happening.

In any situation and equipped with some real evidence you can:

■ identify the scale of the problem yourself;
■ convince your manager that you have a problem which you cannot solve on your own.

We'll look at this in detail later in the workbook.

To sum up, we can say that you can tackle problems of costs on three fronts:

■ keep down costs which are within your control;
■ get value for money for costs which you can't control directly;
■ keep records of cost problems which you have identified but can't influence without support.

Self-assessment 1

1 Identify the differences between direct and indirect materials costs.

_____

_____

_____

2 Claire runs a local newspaper. She pays her advertising sales staff on a commission-only basis and her reporters are given a weekly wage. Are the different forms of wages fixed or variable costs?

■ the wages of the advertising sales staff are _____ _____

■ the wages of the reporters are _____ _____

3 Fill in the missing words in the following sentences.

a Direct labour costs _____ be _____ allocated to a particular product.

b Wages which _____ be allocated to a particular product are _____ labour costs.

c Direct labour costs are often _____ costs because they increase or decrease in proportion to the production being carried out.

15

4 Sam is a first line manager in a factory assembling computer hard disks. Tick the costs which would be under Sam's control and those which would not.

	Controllable	Not controllable
■ wastage of components used in the production of hard disks	☐	☐
■ advertising costs of hard disks	☐	☐
■ Sam's basic salary	☐	☐

Answers to these questions can be found on page 71.

8 Summary

- Profit = Sales − Costs.

- Costs are broadly made up of **labour costs**, **materials costs** and **overheads**.

- Labour costs have to be divided into:

  - direct labour costs – which can be totally allocated to time spent making a particular product or providing a service;
  - indirect labour costs – which are allocated to work other than making a product or directly providing a service.

- Materials costs include:

  - purchasing price of materials;
  - holding costs;
  - reorder costs;
  - stock-out costs.

  Materials costs, like labour costs, have to be divided into direct and indirect materials costs.

- Costs which relate to supporting the main activity are called overheads.
- Costs can be identified as:

  - **variable** – varying with output;
  - **fixed** – incurred regardless of output.

- To control costs:

  - continually monitor costs within your control;
  - get value for money from costs you cannot directly control;
  - keep records of costs you cannot control without support.

Session B Standard costing

1 Introduction

You know that it is useful to control costs. But how do you know you are controlling the right ones? And by how much should you reduce them? You can switch lights off and turn down the heating but your workteam are unlikely to work well in the cold and dark.

It helps you to control anything – the output of a machine or a workteam for instance – if there is a standard against which to measure performance.

In cost control, the first step is to decide what the costs should be and then control what happens in such a way that we meet those 'target' costs. If actual costs of the operation turn out to be different from the expected figure, then we look at the variances and find out why they are different. Then we can decide what action should be taken to bring them back to target.

In this session we will look at different standards and how to use them to control costs.

2 Setting standards

Standard costs are concerned with individual units. Each item of production or service, for instance, will have a standard cost.

A standard cost is a predetermined cost which is achieved by setting standards related to particular circumstances or conditions of work.

A standard cost should indicate not just what a particular cost is **expected** to be, but also what it **ought** to be under certain conditions.

Costs change over time so standards should be reviewed regularly to ensure that they are still relevant.

You can apply standard costs to all the costs in the workplace. These may include:

- direct labour;
- direct materials;
- overheads (fixed and variable).

A mechanic may, for example, be expected to complete the servicing of a car in an hour and this will involve one hour's direct labour cost plus a direct materials cost for, say, oil filter, lubricants and other replacement parts.

17

2.1 Standard cost rates

Standard cost rates are estimated by taking all sorts of considerations into account.

Activity 13

5 mins

a Jot down **two** things which you would take into account in estimating materials costs for something which will be used extensively in your workplace for the next year.

_____

_____

b Write down **two** matters you would have to take into account in estimating labour costs for a forthcoming period.

_____

_____

a I hope you have thought of taking the following into account in respect of materials costs:

■ the purchase price;
■ any expected change (for instance, you might know that the price of oil or computer disks was going to increase);
■ any discount you could negotiate.

b The following, among others, would be relevant for labour costs:

■ the current hourly rate/piece rate;
■ likely trade union agreements on pay rises;
■ other costs, such as overtime premiums, bonuses, employer's national insurance contributions.

Now let's look at performance standards.

2.2 Standard performance rates

To use a standard costing system, somebody must decide:

- the quantities, types and mix of materials to produce any given product;
- the amount and type of labour to produce any given product or service.
  These technical standards are usually set by specialists and involve techniques such as method study and job evaluation.

Two types of standard are commonly used:

- ideal standards;
- expected standards.

Ideal standards are based on perfect working conditions. However, conditions are seldom perfect, often for reasons outside our immediate control. Ideal standards can help to highlight major variances but people tend to find them rather discouraging, because the targets may be too high.

Much better, usually, are **expected standards**. These could well be called realistic standards, as they build in an allowance for an acceptable level of inefficiency. If the workteam is well managed and willing to co-operate, expected standards should be attainable.

Portfolio of evidence B1.1

Activity 14

5 mins

This Activity may provide the basis of appropriate evidence for your S/NVQ portfolio. If you are intending to take this course of action, it might be better to write your answers on separate sheets of paper.

Identify three causes for breaks in production or delivery of service which are not planned and which your workteam has experienced. Suggest changes which you could recommend to your manager to address such situations.

_____

_____

_____

_____

_____

_____

Certain planned breaks are important to allow staff to eat and rest physically and mentally. There are, though, breaks which can occur unexpectedly, such as:

■   when equipment breaks down. A hairdresser may have spare cutting equipment to call upon but if a baker's oven breaks down, replacement may not be possible. A rapid service and repair contract is essential.

■   where the organization runs out of stock and production ceases. Plans for alternative work so that employees have something to do would avoid unnecessary costs, or alternative stockholding policies could be employed.

■   when accidents or injuries occur. Good health and safety training and procedures should limit this problem.

2.3   Standard costing and non-manufacturing organizations

A full standard costing system is less common in organizations which provide a service rather than manufacture something, but many industries, nevertheless, find it useful to set performance standards in order to:

■   measure actual performance;
■   base costs upon them.

For example, a building contractor might base costs on standard performances for:

■   cubic yards of earth excavated per hour by a mechanical digger;
■   lorry loads of earth shifted per day;
■   bricks laid per hour.

Activity 15

3 mins

In an office you will find clerks, word processing operators and typists at work. And the manager may spend a lot of time talking to clients in a separate office.

Suggest two possible performance standards which you could set if you were in charge in this situation

_____

_____

You could set performance standards for:

- letters typed per hour by a typist or word processing operator;
- percentage completion of correct invoices;
- number of deals by the manager per day.

3 Standard costing in practice

Now let's put standard costing into operation in the following Activity.

Activity 16

Plastiform plc makes a range of plastic furniture. A standard costing system is in operation. The following information is available for one product – plastic tables.

The raw material (plastic) has been costed at £6.10 per metre. The standard usage of material is reckoned to be 5 metres per table.

Two types of labour are required in the production process: moulders and cutters.

- The standard rate for moulders is £4.00 per hour.
- The standard rate for cutters is £5.00 per hour.
- The expected standard for moulders is 1½ hours per table.
- The expected standard for cutters is 2½ hours per table.

Complete the standard cost sheet below to show what the standard cost will be for a table.

Standard cost sheet

Direct materials: 5 metres at £6.10 _____ = £_____

Direct wages:

Moulder _____ hours × £_____ = £6.00

Cutter _____ hours × £_____ = _____

_____

The answer to this Activity can be found on page 72.

Now let's see how differences in actual costs (variances) can be analysed.

4 Variances from standard

Variances are the differences between what costs or revenue **actually are** and what they **should be** – the standard.

A variance can be either **adverse** (when the actual cost is higher than the standard) or **favourable** (when the cost is actually lower than the standard).

With a sound standard costing system, variances can be highlighted for:

■ every raw material used;
■ every type of direct labour;
■ all overheads.

Clearly, this detailed information is very important to managers.

The following diagrams show how an analysis of variances breaks down.

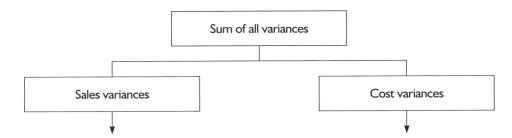

Sales variances can be further broken down to:

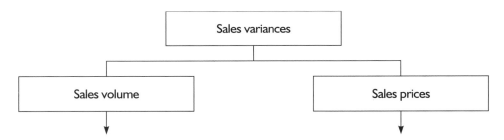

And cost variances can be broken down:

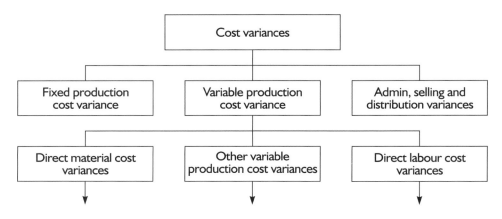

An analysis of materials and labour costs illustrates that standard costing can help pinpoint variances and so improve control.

4.1 Direct material cost variances

Direct material cost variances can be divided into two types:

- usage variance;
- price variance.

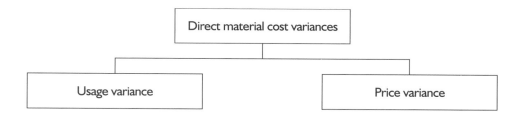

If an adverse usage variance occurs, it means that more material has been used than the standard indicated. This might have come about because inefficient methods meant that more scrap than expected was produced.

Activity 17

A decision to improve a price variance by using cheaper materials can lead to more scrap and a worsening usage variance. The consequences of changes made in response to variances need careful consideration.

Who do you think is ultimately responsible for a usage variance?

_____

Who do you think is directly responsible for excessive scrap being produced?

_____

Ultimately, the production controller, or similarly named person, is responsible. However, the first line manager is likely to have to account directly for scrap being higher than expected.

Now let's look at the direct labour cost variance.

4.2 Direct labour cost variances

Direct labour cost variances break down to:

- efficiency variance;
- idle time variance;
- rate variance.

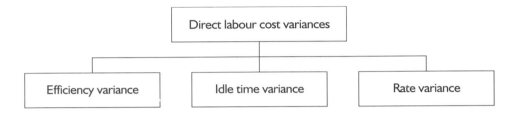

An adverse efficiency variance means that the workteam spent longer making the product than the standard indicated. Once again, we would need to know who was responsible and the reasons for the standard not being achieved.

An idle time variance – often called cost time variance – is caused by the workteam not having any work for a longer period than expected.

This could be caused, among other reasons, by:

- equipment breakdown;
- materials hold-up;
- a lack of power.

Activity 18

Suggest who or what you think would be responsible for each of these causes.

Equipment breakdown _____

Materials hold-up _____

Lack of power_____

EXTENSION 3
Calculating variances can be time-consuming. Computerization is often used in practice to provide us with variance information. This extension shows how a spreadsheet can be used to help us with costing for materials, labour and overheads in Section 3 of *Drury's Management and Cost Accounting Spreadsheet Applications Manual.*

In practice, things are often more complicated than they seem. There could be a number of contributory factors which different managers would have to account for. It's quite possible that you have suggested people who would be responsible, say:

- for equipment breakdown, maintenance engineer;
- materials hold-up, purchasing;
- lack of power, interruption of power supply owing to adverse weather conditions.

An analysis of variances from standard costs can lead to a very detailed and far-reaching investigation of the problem. Perhaps you've already been involved in such investigations.

Identifying the responsible people is not a witch hunt; we are not looking for somebody to blame. The important step is to account for the variance so that better control can be established in future.

Self-assessment 2

1 Complete the following definition by filling in the missing words.

A standard cost is a _____ cost which is achieved by setting _____ related to particular circumstances or conditions of work.

2 Identify two reasons for setting performance standards.

_____

_____

3 Calculate the standard cost of a vase using the following information.

■ Glass is used which costs £8.00 per metre. A quarter of a metre is used for one vase.
■ A glassworker is paid £5 per hour and can make ten vases in an hour.

Standard cost sheet

Direct materials: _____

Direct wages: _____

_____

---

4 Identify the variances comprising:

■ direct material cost variances

_____

_____

■ direct labour cost variances

_____

_____

5 State what is indicated by favourable and adverse variances.

_____

_____

_____

_____

Answers to these questions can be found on page 71.

5 Summary

- A standard cost is a cost calculated in advance and based on certain approved, specified work practices.

- Standard costing allows management to pinpoint variances precisely.

- Standard costs have two elements.

  - costs;
  - performance level.

- Standard performance levels should be based on expected standards and contain an allowable level of slack.

- Analysis of cost variances can lead to better cost control.

- The complete diagram of variances we have discussed is as shown below:

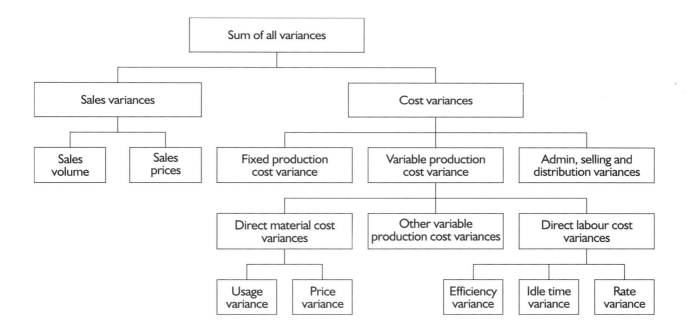

Session C Controlling costs in the workplace

1 Introduction

You know what costs are and appreciate the ones important in your workplace. But do you control them well enough? If something goes wrong, you or your manager will have some explaining to do.

Information about costs is necessary before almost any important management decision can be made. The process of collecting that information will often start with you, the first line manager. The more you know and understand about costs in your workplace, the easier it will be for you to answer questions, anticipate problems and exercise control.

Let's begin by looking at some examples of the sorts of decisions I mean which lead to particular cost information being important. We will then go on to look at monitoring and control of those costs later in the session.

2 Cost information and decisions

Here are three questions asking for information about costs before a management decision can be made in each case.

Activity 19

Jot down what you think could be the kind of decision which will arise from information given in answer to each of the questions.

■ How many units of a proposed new product are likely to be sold and what are the fixed costs? Once this question is answered you could use the information to help you decide

_____

_____

■ How much does it cost to feed a patient in hospital for a week (a) using the hospital kitchen, (b) using an outside caterer? The answer to this question might lead the hospital authorities to investigate

_____

_____

_____

■ Can coal from a certain mine be sold at more or less than the cost of extracting it? No further changes to working practices are possible. The answer to this question might lead to

_____

_____

_____

> Research by Berliner and Brimson in 1988 identified that the most effective cost control concentrated on the design rather than the other stages of a product life. It is at that early stage of decision making and planning that later costs are determined.

In the first instance, by knowing the fixed costs and a good estimation of likely sales you can work out how the fixed costs can be divided per unit sold which will help in then setting a price per unit to provide a profit. This is a pricing decision.

In the second instance, hospital authorities can investigate whether it is cheaper to use their own kitchens and staff or to buy in the services of an outside caterer. There may well be things other than costs, such as the need to meet specific dietary needs or deal with rapidly changing volumes of patients, which affect the decision. This is a 'make or buy' decision.

Finally, coal mines in which the costs of extraction exceed the selling price have been closed down because they are unprofitable. As with the earlier decisions, costs will not be the only things looked at, as making whole communities redundant can have political implications, but they will be important. This is a closure decision.

The three kinds of decisions we have looked at – pricing, 'make or buy' and closure – are major decisions made in a wide range of industries. Without collecting information about costs on a regular basis, organizations may not even know whether a particular process makes a profit or runs at a loss, or whether it would be cheaper for them to make something themselves or buy it in. Costs and cost information are important to managers making a wide range of decisions.

2.1 Cost statements

A cost statement is often used to show the breakdown of costs so that the final cost of a product or service can be analysed.

Let's begin by looking at a manufacturing example. It's helpful in manufacturing to identify another cost – the **total factory cost**. This includes all the **prime** or direct costs plus all the indirect costs arising out of the need to keep the factory (but not the offices) running. Indirect costs are **factory overheads**.

Activity 20

5 mins

Write down one example of an appropriate cost beside each item shown in the following cost statement for the production of a car. I've given examples of factory overheads to help.

Cost statement of a car			
	£	£	Example of appropriate cost
Direct material		2000	
Direct labour		1500	
Prime cost		3500	
Factory overheads		2000	Lighting, heating, health and safety expenditure
Total factory cost		5500	
Administrative overheads	1000		
Selling and distribution overheads (including dealer's profit margin)	1500	2500	
Total costs		8000	
Profit		1000	
Selling price		£9000	

Of course, you could have thought of all sorts of things, since the manufacture, selling and distribution of a car is a complex process involving many people.

Under the prime costs heading, you could have identified any of the raw materials which go into a car and the wages of anybody directly involved in production.

Administration could be anything to do with purchasing, payments or any of the paperwork involved in running a business.

Selling and distribution would include advertising, promotions, the cost of delivering cars to the dealers and getting them in showroom condition.

Now let's see how this sort of analysis can be used if we adapt it slightly for an organization, such as a hospital, which provides a service.

We'll say it costs about £350 a week to keep a patient in hospital.

	£	£	Examples
Cost structure of patient care (cost per in-patient week)			
Direct labour		140	Medical and nursing salaries
Direct materials		40	Drugs, medical supplies
Prime cost		180	
Administrative overheads	50		Clerical salaries, rates, telephone
General hospital overheads	120	170	Catering, cleaning costs and maintenance
Total costs		£350	

Once again, the costs are broken down into direct costs and overheads.

2.2 Cost units

Costs can be divided into direct costs and overheads. However, this analysis is only useful if the costs relate to an identifiable item, called a *cost unit*. In the example of the cost of producing a car, the car was the cost unit. Each firm defines its own cost units.

The most obvious cost unit is the finished product.

For instance, a brewery may send out its beer in barrels or kegs which would be the cost units. A cement factory will probably send its cement out by the tonne, so will probably use a tonne of cement as a cost unit.

Cost units can be used by organizations which provide a service too.

Activity 21

Jot down what you think might be the cost units used by:

■ swimming baths

_____

■ a school canteen

_____

■ the Post Office

_____

Swimming baths would probably use the number of bathers as a cost unit, and a school canteen could use individual meals produced as a cost unit. The Post Office is a more difficult problem. You could have suggested an individual letter or package for the sorting office, a customer for counter staff or an individual address for delivery staff.

Relating costs to the final unit produced enables us to make comparisons to see how well we are performing.

Activity 22

4 mins

What comparisons might we make which would help us to judge our performance?

Write down two suggestions.

_____

_____

Perhaps you suggested:

- comparing performance over several years;
- comparing actual costs with planned costs;
- comparing your own costs with those of your competitors.

This list is not comprehensive and you may well have thought of other possibilities.

As well as identifying the cost of the final product or final service, a business can also analyse any part of the workplace and work out appropriate cost units. For example, some of the cost units we might find in a car factory are:

- final product – cost per car;
- electricity cost – cost per kilowatt hour;
- computer running cost – cost per computer minute of operation;
- canteen – cost per canteen meal.

This leads us to the subject of cost centres.

3 Cost centres

A cost centre is a location where costs can be identified, grouped together and then finally related to a cost unit.

A cost centre is, in other words, a collection point for costs.

By a 'location' we mean something like:

■ a department within a particular workplace;
■ a work area;
■ a machine or group of machines;
■ a person, e.g. a hospital consultant.

The advantages of breaking down costs into a number of cost centres are that:

■ it allows information on costs to be collected more easily;
■ it provides information on costs in different parts of the organization;
■ managers of particular cost centres can be given a budget figure against which costs can be controlled.

Identifying costs in cost centres helps to determine the efficiency of various parts of the organization, and to control how each unit or department spends its money. It would, for instance, enable senior management to make a decision about whether printing should continue to be done internally, or to be contracted to outside suppliers.

The diagram below shows an example of three cost centres within an organization. Each cost centre collects:

■ costs of materials and labour used within the centre;
■ a proportion of the overheads for the whole organization.

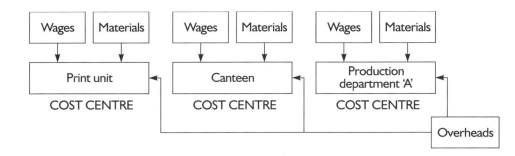

Activity 23

3
mins

Look at the above and decide into which cost centres you would collect the following costs:

Paper for photocopiers _____

Cook's wages _____

Wages of machine operator working in Department A _____

_____

It looks as though paper for the photocopier is a print unit cost; the cook's wages are a canteen cost, and the machine operator's wages are a cost incurred in production Department A. Each cost centre would collect the costs relevant to it.

In the diagram above, the canteen and the print unit are providing a service to other parts of the organization. So we can distinguish between the two types of cost centre:

■ service centres, and
■ product centres.

An important aim of a manufacturing organization is to make goods; that's how it earns its income. All services (such as the canteen, the stores, the maintenance department and so on) exist only to assist in that aim. Therefore, all costs must be finally transferred from the service centres to the product centres.

For a building firm, the total cost of building houses is made up of many different individual costs. If the firm provides safety helmets for its workers, the cost of the helmets may be initially part of the materials costs for a 'safety department' cost centre. Ultimately these costs must appear in the cost of each house.

In a nursing home, general cleaning costs and office expenses would ultimately be charged against the costs of looking after each resident.

3.1 Cost codes

A good cost system enables costs to be:

■ collected;
■ analysed;
■ controlled.

This means that we have to be able to find out precisely what expenses have been incurred in any part of the workplace, and we have to know how much we are spending in the workplace as a whole on different sorts of expense (overtime, electricity, stationery, etc.).

To help us do this a system of cost codes is often used.

This will mean having two types of code:

■ a special code for each cost centre which will identify any costs incurred in that cost centre;
■ a special code for each cost or group of costs wherever they occur throughout the workplace. (Stationery, for instance, will have the same code wherever it occurs.)

By combining the cost centre code (accounts, for example) and the code identifying the type of cost (say, stationery), we can identify how much has been spent on any particular item or group of items in any particular cost centres, and so control costs throughout the organization.

Let's look at how a cost coding system works.

Each workplace uses certain groups of numbers to mean particular things. These groups usually contain enough spare numbers for new kinds of cost to be added to the list of codes. For instance, a workplace which starts with seven different cost centres may allocate the group of codes 01, 02, 03, . . ., 18, 19 to cost centres, providing plenty of room to expand the list.

Let's look at the example of likely cost codes for a general hospital.

Hospital cost centres	Codes	Items of expenditure	Codes
Ward 1	001	Nursing sister's salary	025
Ward 2	002	Staff nurse's salary	026
Ward 3	003	Cleaner's wages	107
Theatre 1	098	Medical equipment	400–449
Theatre 2	099	Drugs	450–500
Pharmacy	171	Laundry assistant's wages	181
Physiotherapy department	264	Cleaning materials	600–630
Laundry	351	Cook's wages	197
Canteen	400		

Sister's salary on Ward 2 will be coded 002 025. Cleaning materials for Ward 3 could be coded 003 610 or 003 622 or 003 630 because the range indicates different codes for different types of cleaning materials.

Activity 24

5 mins

It is important for cost codes to be clear and well understood for them to be effective. A code for 'sundry expenses' is often overused.

Derive codes for the following. Where you have a range of numbers, choose any one within that range.

- Theatre 1 staff nurse's salary _____ _____

- Theatre 2 medical equipment _____ _____

- Physiotherapy department medical equipment _____ _____

- Drug coded 459 and ordered for the pharmacy _____ _____

- Canteen cook's wages _____ _____

The answer to this Activity can be found on page 73.

Activity 25

2 mins

Here is a list of some costs in the hospital to which cost codes have been allocated. One of them seems rather suspicious and would need to be checked out. (Tick the suspect code.)

098 107 ☐

001 026 ☐

400 457 ☐

According to these cost codes, the canteen has been ordering drugs (400 457)! This sounds very unlikely and needs investigating.

A system of cost codes means that everybody in the workplace describes each kind of cost in the same way. Information about costs is simplified and is presented in a standard way making it easier to interpret and analyse.

Cost codes, made up of cost centre code and type of cost code, also mean that every single cost can be traced to a certain cost centre, improving control.

Identifying certain kinds of expense by the same code throughout the workplace means that you can also see how much you are spending on certain things (overtime or electricity, for instance), overall. This will help in deciding how to best utilize resources or to economize.

4 Control through cost centres

Whether that cost centre is a work area, a machine or a group of machines or a team of people, it could well be you, as first line manager, who is responsible for maintaining the cost centre and the associated costs.
You might have to:

■ requisition materials;
■ authorize and collect time sheets;
■ control the level of costs in your work area.

Each of these are associated with materials, wages or overheads.

Let's look at how materials and wages costs are collected in appropriate cost centres and applied to units produced in the workplace.

The collection and application of overhead costs is rather more complex, but we'll look at that later.

4.1 Cost centres and materials costs

The materials cost of any product will come from:

■ purchases bought directly from an outside supplier;
■ stock issued from the workplace stores.

A first line manager may have the responsibility for:

■ raising a materials requisition for goods in the stores which are needed for the job;
■ raising a purchase requisition for goods needed for the job, which are not in the stores;
■ taking care of materials once they are in the work area.

The next diagram shows an outline of the movement of paperwork and goods which take place when goods are requested.

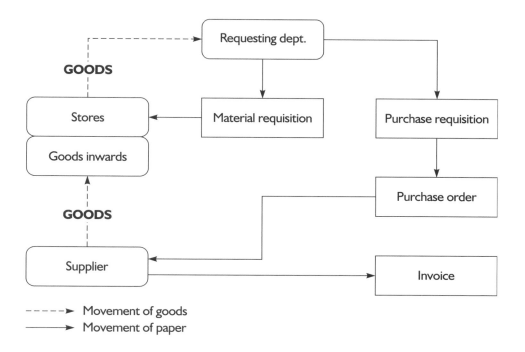

- - - - ▶ Movement of goods
———————▶ Movement of paper

Activity 26

Look at the diagram and identify three people or departments, apart from the requesting department, who have a part to play in the materials costing system.

Against each one write down briefly what you think their responsibilities are.

_____

_____

_____

_____

_____

_____

Here is my breakdown of the roles played by various departments in the materials costing system.

- Purchasing department:

  - ordering goods;
  - keeping lists of approved suppliers;
  - checking suppliers' prices.

- Goods inward department:

  - receiving goods;
  - checking quality and quantity of goods supplied;
  - issuing goods received notes to accounts department.

- Stores department:

  - storage and care of goods in store;
  - keeping records of receipts and issues to and from stores and current balances of items held;
  - issuing purchase requisitions when stock levels fall to reorder level;
  - issuing supplies for certain jobs on receipt of a proper materials requisition note.

- Accounting/costing department

  - receiving and checking invoices against orders and goods received notes;
  - keeping accounting records for the entire workplace;
  - paying the supplier;
  - costing materials for particular jobs;
  - entering cost details on cost sheets.

A typical materials requisition note would look like this, although, of course, they vary in minor details from one workplace to another.

Materials Requisition Note				
Date required 1.7.96			Cost centre Assembly shop Job number 41	
Description	Item code	Quantity	Unit cost	Amount
Copper Brackets	A 468	30	£15.00	£450.00
Signature of requisitioning manager/supervisor		A.N.Body		Date 15.6.96

4.2 Cost centres and labour costs

You are likely to be directly involved in the control and recording of labour costs. Your position gives you a degree of authority over your workteam and responsibility for:

- controlling timekeeping, particularly important if you are monitoring a flexi-time system;
- controlling quality of performance;
- recording time spent on individual jobs;
- passing time records to the appropriate department for analysis.

Other departments which will be involved to some extent in the labour costing system are:

- wages department;
- accounts costing department;
- personnel department.

A clock card, time sheets or similar forms to record time spent at work are used to help in the calculation of labour costs.

Clock Card							
Name *A Brown*						Employee no. *740*	
Department (cost centre) *Assembly shop*						Week ending *25/6*	
	AM		PM		Excess hours		
Date	In	Out	In	Out	In	Out	Total hours
21/6	*7.58*	*12.01*	*1.00*	*5.01*			*8.00*
22/6	*7.55*	*12.00*	*1.00*	*5.05*			*8.00*
23/6	*8.00*	*12.00*	*1.00*	*5.00*	*6.00*	*9.00*	*11.00*
24/6	*7.55*	*12.00*	*1.00*	*4.55*			*8.00*
25/6	*7.59*	*12.01*	*1.02*	*5.00*			*8.00*

The clock card, illustrated above, has to be analysed before being passed to the wages department.

Activity 27

5 mins

Using the information on our example of a clock card, fill in the blank spaces below, assuming a normal working week of 40 hours.

Regular time _____ hours at £6.00   £ _____

Overtime   _____ hours at £9.00   £ _____

Gross earnings   £ _____

The answer to this Activity can be found on page 73.

The team leader is usually directly responsible for confirming that the records of how the workteam's time has been spent are true. In a flexi-time system appropriate core time must be confirmed (i.e. employees should be at work when required) as well as attending for the appropriate total time within the flexible working pattern. But the team leader's responsibilities for labour cost control don't end here.

Typical responsibilities would include:

- allocating time to individual jobs;
- allocating an appropriate grade of staff to a particular job;
- controlling the amount of time spent on individual jobs by members of the workteam;
- keeping idle time, such as travel time, to a minimum.

To these we can add the 'paperwork responsibilities' which go with the job:

- verifying job costs (confirming that details shown on job cards are correct);
- passing job costs to the costing department for analysis;
- verifying idle time costs;
- passing details of idle time costs to the costing department so that it can be properly accounted for. Generally it needs to be apportioned on some reasonable basis over all jobs.

The job card, work ticket, or a computer printout used to analyse time and services provided, are key documents in transferring labour cost information from a particular work area to whoever is responsible for costing.

> Cost control is only worthwhile if it saves more for an organization than the costs of its operation. Too much time or paperwork and you should question its relevance.

It's important that the information shown on the various documents which relate to labour costs balances.

The presentation of information about time for labour purposes obviously varies from one workplace to another but this example shows you the most important features.

Work Ticket						
Employee no.	740	Date	22/6	Job no.	41	
Operation	Drilling	Account	Work in progress	Dept.	Assembly shop	
Time started	4.00	Rate	£6.00	Pieces:		
Time completed	4.45	Amount	£4.50	Worked	20	
Signed	A Brown			Rejected	–	
Verified	A N Body (Supervisor)			Completed	20	

Activity 28

How long did the workteam member spend on job 41?

_____

How much did he get paid for job 41?

_____

You probably worked out that job 41, to which this work ticket relates, took 45 minutes. Since the hourly rate for the job is £6.00, the workteam member will be paid £4.50.

Now let's have a look for a moment at the question of idle time.

Common causes are:

- equipment breakdown;
- power failure;
- waiting for work to be scheduled;
- waiting for materials or tools;
- waiting for instructions.

Idle time is not normally charged directly against the job, but is regarded as a production overhead, or overhead incurred in providing a service. If the fault can be traced to one particular department, it may be charged against that department.

For instance, say a maintenance programme, scheduled to be completed during the fortnight in July of factory shut-down, runs late and production time is lost once everybody is back at work.

It seems obvious that in this case the fault can be traced back to the maintenance department and the cost will be charged to it. In that case the first line manager in the maintenance department has got some explaining to do.

Activity 29

2 mins

From what we've said so far, which department or individual do you think will receive all the documents relating to labour costs, including:

- clock cards;
- time sheets;
- job cards;
- analysis of idle time?

I hope we can agree that it is the costing department we're talking about, if one exists, or it may be a departmental manager's job to:

- maintain job cost sheets for each job;
- analyse total wages between various cost centres.

4.3 Cost centres and overheads

The first problem we come across is that some overheads belong entirely to one cost centre, whilst some can be shared among several cost centres.

Where an overhead can belong entirely to one cost centre we say that it is **allocated** to the appropriate cost centre. The first line manager of that cost centre will bear the responsibility for controlling these overhead costs within the cost centre.

Activity 30

Think of two overhead costs from your own workplace which could be allocated entirely to one cost centre.

_____

_____

It's unlikely that we've thought of the same things but here are a couple of examples which spring to mind:

■ the wages of a manager in the food hall of a large superstore will be allocated to the food hall cost centre;
■ the cost of an advertising promotion will be allocated to the marketing cost centre.

Activity 31

Here are some more overhead costs, similar in that they can be allocated entirely to individual cost centres. Against each one, write down which of the following three classes of overheads it belongs to – production overheads, administration overheads or selling and distribution overheads.

■ Wages of managers working entirely within a particular production department.

_____

■ Paint, oil and grease used in a certain production department.

_____

- Wages of switchboard operators and receptionists.

- Travelling expenses of sales staff.

The first two costs are production overheads, the wages of switchboard operators and receptionists are likely to be an administrative overhead and the travelling expenses of the sales staff are a selling overhead. Each of these could be allocated directly and entirely to one cost centre.

Often, though, overhead costs have to be spread over a number of cost centres. These costs are controlled first of all in one cost centre and then **apportioned** between other cost centres, using an agreed method of deciding how they should be shared out or apportioned.

Here are some overhead costs which might be apportioned among various departments. I've also shown the cost centre where the cost would initially be controlled and suggested a possible method for apportioning the cost between departments.

Type of cost	Cost centre where cost is initially controlled	Possible method of apportionment
Rent and rates	Property manager	Area occupied by various departments
Lighting and heating	Plant engineer	Volume occupied by various departments
Insurance of equipment	Company secretary	Value of equipment in various departments

Activity 32

5 mins

In the space provided below, write down which cost centre you think should initially control each overhead and suggest a method by which they could fairly be apportioned.

Type of cost	Cost centre where cost is initially controlled	Possible method of apportionment
Staff welfare		
Advertising for staff		
Building repairs		

Where possible it is preferable to **allocate** overheads directly to cost centres, if there are clear and agreed bases for doing so rather than to **apportion** them between cost centres, as the overheads are identified as being generated by, or the responsibility of, those cost centres.

Here are my suggestions. You may have thought of other equally reasonable suggestions, so don't feel that our answers have to be the same.

Type of cost	Cost centre where cost is initially controlled	Possible method of apportionment
Staff welfare	Personnel manager	Number of staff per department
Advertising for staff	Personnel manager	Number of vacancies notified per department
Building repairs	Building and works manager	Floor area per department

There is no hard-and-fast method of apportioning overheads. But methods should be logical.

4.4 Transferring costs from service centres to product centres

As you know, all costs have finally to be transferred to the departments which actually produce the goods or carry out the service.

Activity 33

Suggest to which department or work area costs might finally be transferred in these two examples.

■ In a factory manufacturing electronic toys.

_____

■ In a garage which services cars.

_____

We may not have used quite the same names for the departments concerned, but I would say that costs in the toy factory have to be transferred to the production department. In the garage, costs have to be transferred to the repair shop floor (since this, rather than stores for example, is where the actual service to the customer takes place).

For the purposes of control, we will have collected costs in a number of cost centres throughout the workplace, both product centres and service centres. The service centre costs must be transferred to product centres.

Making this transfer can be quite complex. Put simply, you transfer costs from service centres to product centres according to how much work or time has been given by the service department to the product department. These then appear as overheads in the product departments.

So stores (a service department) may transfer its costs to production departments on the basis of the number of materials requisitions made.

Activity 34

Suggest how another service department, maintenance, might transfer its costs to production departments.

_____

_____

One way would be to transfer maintenance costs on the basis of the number of hours of maintenance work done for the various departments.

Suppose, in a certain workplace, 30,000 material requisitions are made to stores and stores' costs amount to £12,000.

- Department A makes 20,000 requisitions.
- Department B makes 10,000 requisitions.

Department A, having made two-thirds of the requisitions, will be charged with £8000 or two-thirds of the stores' costs. Department B, having made one-third of the requisitions on stores, will be charged with one-third of the stores' costs or £4000.

Activity 35

The maintenance department does 5000 hours' work for Department A and 1000 hours for Department B, a total of 6000 hours. Maintenance department overhead costs are £18,000. How much will be charged to Department A and Department B from the maintenance department?

- Department A: 5/6 × £18,000 = £ _____
- Department B: 1/6 × £18,000 = £ _____

The answer to this Activity can be found on page 73.

It is not necessary for you to know more about the accounting process of transferring costs. It is this awareness of costs, not accounting manipulations, which is the key to success. Cost consciousness is important managerial behaviour. So, in the next session we'll consider how to foster a cost-conscious attitude.

Self-assessment 3

1 a Name the two types of cost included in prime cost.

_____

_____

b What additional costs are added to prime cost to arrive at the total factory cost?

_____

2 State what is meant by a cost centre.

_____

3 Identify the three characteristics of a good cost system.

_____

_____

_____

4 What are the two main functions of the costing department as far as labour costs are concerned?

_____

_____

5 Briefly explain the difference between allocation and apportionment.

_____

_____

_____

_____

_____

Answers to these questions can be found on page 72.

5 Summary

- Managers need cost information to make decisions.

- Direct costs are related to the individual unit produced, e.g. cost of raw materials.

- Overhead costs cannot be directly attributed to any one unit of production or service provided.

- Cost units are identifiable items against which the costs of a company, department or other defined part of the organization can be related.

- A cost coding systems can be used for tracking every cost in the workplace.

- Cost centres are locations where costs can be conveniently collected and grouped.

- Costing provides for budgetary control and product or service costing.

- Direct material and labour costs are collected in cost centres and charged directly to the job. Overheads are also applied to job costs; many are estimates.

- Costing departments process cost data and provide cost statements.

Session D Cost consciousness at work

1 Introduction

We've seen that controlling and keeping down costs demands continued effort. You have to be permanently on the look-out for performance levels falling, materials and equipment being wrongly used, bottlenecks, idle time, untidy and slipshod ways of working and so on.

Clearly you can only do so much yourself.

You need the support of the workteam in looking for and maintaining ways of keeping down costs, and in keeping records of what is actually happening in your work areas.

If one person tries to keep costs down on their own by turning off lights when they go out, it will have little effect. But if that person can persuade a dozen others to do the same, increasing amounts can be saved.

So what can we do to make the workteam aware of the costs and become enthusiastic about keeping them down?

We will look at ways of communicating the importance of costs in this session.

Portfolio of evidence B1.2	Activity 36	4 mins

This Activity may provide the basis of evidence for your S/NVQ portfolio. If you are intending to take this course of action, it might be better to write your answers on separate sheets of paper.

Suggest two ways in which you think you could make your workteam more cost conscious. How would you implement your suggestions?

_____

_____

_____

_____

Typical answers might include:

- getting the workteam more involved;
- encouraging them to make suggestions;
- offering prizes for suggestions on how to keep costs down;
- passing on information about costs;
- telling them when costs increase or decrease.

Perhaps you might talk to your workteam or put up notices and then follow up with meetings, discussions and so on.

If you are compiling an S/NVQ portfolio you may be able to use notices and testimony from your workteam members and your manager as the basis of possible acceptable evidence.

The three keys to success are:

- **Involvement**

- **Communication**

- **Feedback**

2 Involvement and communication

Controlling costs in the workplace is often a matter of observation and common sense, of noticing clues and following them up.

Cost consciousness means treating costs in the workplace as though your money was going to be used to pay for them. Successfully finding ways of keeping costs down means keeping an eye on your spending all the time rather than looking for one good idea. In the end your job and the money you earn depend on a successful operation, of which controlling costs is an important element.

We need to communicate with people about cost if we want them to become involved. The trouble is, much of the information used in the workplace to monitor costs is likely to be in the form of financial statements which are not easy to understand and which can easily put people off.

You and other team leaders need to give their team members information about costs in terms that are relevant, timely and in an appropriate place.

Activity 37

Here are two ways of communicating information about a quarterly electricity bill.

Tick whichever you think would make you more conscious of the cost of the electricity you are using.

(a) ☐

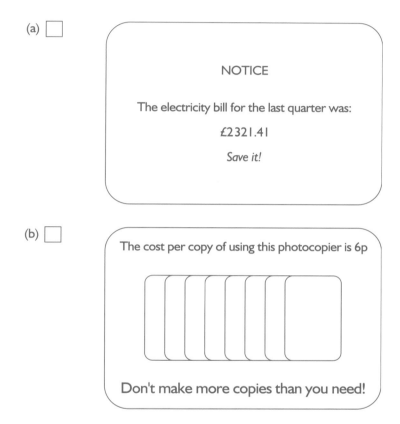

NOTICE

The electricity bill for the last quarter was:

£2321.41

Save it!

(b) ☐

The cost per copy of using this photocopier is 6p

Don't make more copies than you need!

We can make a case for saying that either of these would be effective for different people. Let's look at (a) first.

Sometimes the sheer size of a sum of money, like the cost of this electricity bill, can give people a jolt. £2321.41 sounds a lot more serious than 6p per photocopied sheet.

However, large figures quickly baffle us and tend not to mean a lot to us. Electricity bills of £1500, £2400 or £13,967 all sound equally terrifying if our quarterly bill at home is about £75.

It's all too easy to feel that such a large sum is nothing to do with us. We didn't contribute much to the bill in the first place and there is nothing we can do to reduce it.

Knowing that each photocopy we take costs 6p is likely to make a bigger impression, because it relates directly to what we are doing, particularly if we have to use a counter which charges copies directly to our budget.

So, I would say that as a piece of information (b) is likely to make people more aware of the costs and likely to try to do something about them than (a).

This sort of information doesn't just have to be in the form of some kind of notice. Just saying something like:

'This aluminium wrapper is £50 a roll now. I don't think we should let it get knocked about.'

or

'We've just spent £200 having these blades reset. Better make sure that no grit gets in there.'

may have a similar effect.

Activity 38

2 mins

Refer back to the two notices about costs.

Which do you think is a more effective place to display the information these notices contain – the canteen notice-board or the photocopier?

_____

Information about costs will make more impact if provided where the cost is about to be incurred and just as it's going to be incurred.

What we read as we are about to use a piece of equipment is harder to avoid than information on the canteen notice-board.

Of course, like many notices, we can get used to them in time and fail to see them. It is useful to replace them with new and different, but striking, notices regularly.

We can say that information about costs needs to be:

■ in a form we can relate to;
■ at the time and place the cost is incurred.

2.1 Feedback

Now let's look at feedback – the response we give to the workteam's efforts to keep costs down or to their suggestions for cost savings.

Activity 39

3 mins

Suppose somebody in your workplace suggests a change to a certain process which will reduce costs. The change is approved and made, and there is an article about it in the house newspaper. Write down two important pieces of information which you would hope to find in the article.

_____

_____

You may have had several ideas but I hope among them would be:

■ the name of the person who made the suggestion;
■ how much money it will save.

If we are to be aware of costs, we want to know how much we're saving by our efforts. Certainly, if we're going to maintain an interest in costs, we need to know that we're making progress. And by recognizing who suggested the cost saving, further emphasis is being placed on its importance.

Of course, not all suggestions are necessarily good ideas.

Activity 40

2 mins

Somebody in your workteam suggests changing your computer stationery supplier. He has spoken to a representative of the alternative supplier and obtained some prices. On the face of it, it looks as though the alternative supplier's prices are less than you are currently paying. Investigating further, you find that the prices apply only for larger volume purchases than you would make and that the existing suppliers have a better reputation for quality and reliability.

Tick the appropriate box to indicate if you would:

a let the subject drop because telling your workteam member might discourage him from making further suggestions?   ☐

b tell him that it wasn't a workable idea?   ☐

c thank him for taking the trouble to find out about the alternative supplier and explain why you weren't going to take up the suggestion?   ☐

You probably chose (c).

EXTENSION 4
Chapter 7 of
David Doyle's book
*Cost Control: A
Strategic Guide* looks
at cost responsibility
and awareness in
some depth.

It's easy to understand that even though the suggestion isn't taken up, people need feedback on their ideas if they are to maintain an interest. However, it's not easy to remember to supply that feedback when we're under a lot of pressure to do all sorts of other jobs.

It's worth making the effort, however. If you don't encourage cost consciousness, even when it is not directly useful, it won't be there when you need it.

3 Checklists for keeping costs down

Finding ways of controlling costs and keeping them down depends upon thinking about every situation in the workplace and asking whether we are making the best possible use of the resources involved and doing the task in question in the most efficient way.

The questions we need to ask ourselves and the answers we will get will vary with the job and the workplace.

I hope you will find the following checklists help you to channel your thoughts as you examine your work area to ensure you have your workteam operating efficiently. Use the space provided to make your own notes.

3.1 Checklist for the workteam

■ Do I use people with the right amount of skill for the job in hand?

_____

■ Do I use highly paid people for low level work? If so, why? Can it be avoided?

_____

_____

■ Are salaries reviewed regularly?

_____

■ Is all our overtime necessary?

_____

■ What causes idle time?

  ■ Lack of materials? ☐ _____

  ■ Lack of available equipment? ☐ _____

  ■ Lack of precise instructions? ☐ _____

  ■ Lack of supervision? ☐ _____

- Are the workteam good about timekeeping?

  _____

- Are all the workteam fully trained?

  _____

- Are the workteam fully competent?

  _____

- Do their skills need bringing up to date?

  _____

- Is career development taken seriously?

  _____

- Are they willing to try new ideas?

  _____

- Is there any information they would like to know about the workplace, the organization or the product?

  _____

- How often do I make a point of chatting to them about themselves and the job?

  _____

- Do I ever have to explain what I want done several times?

  _____

- Should I write instructions for any tasks the workteam do?

  _____

- Are written instructions up to date, in the right place and readable?

  _____

- Do I give the workteam feedback on their performance regularly (not just when things go wrong)?

  _____

- What is our absenteeism record like?

  _____

- How many of the workteam have left in the past two years? Why?

  _____

- Have the workteam any special skills or knowledge which we're not using?

  _____

- What records do I keep to help make the best possible use of the workteam?

  _____

57

3.2 Checklist for materials

- Do we use the cheapest materials for the purpose without reducing the quality?

- Do we keep small stocks (sub-stocks) outside the main stores area?

- Do I know about them?

- Are all sub-stocks accounted for?

- Do we run out of materials? Why?

- Do we have any out-of-date stock? Why?

- Are any materials damaged during storage?

- What control have I over:
  - production materials?
  - Consumables – bags, stationery, paper, oil, grease, packing materials, cleaning materials, etc.?

- Is scrap or waste material increasing/decreasing? Is work having to be done again to reach appropriate standards? Why?

- Is the workplace clean and tidy? How often do I check housekeeping?

3.3 Checklist for machines, equipment and services

- Do I report faults as soon as they occur?

  _____

- Do I keep a record of the date and reason for machine failure?

  _____

- Is all our equipment regularly maintained?

  _____

- How fully used is the equipment for which I am responsible?

  _____

- Could we get rid of any out-of-date machines?

  _____

- Can I improve the layout of the equipment in my work area?

  _____

- Are any machines standing idle? Why?

  _____

- Do we switch off lights and power when they are not needed?

  _____

- Do we send faxes overnight whenever possible and reroute calls through a cheaper call provider or use e-mail?

  _____

- What changes would I like to introduce in the way we work which will make us more efficient?

  _____

- Which departments do I need to help me to do this?

  _____

  _____

  _____

Self-assessment 4

1 State the three keys to success in making a workteam more cost conscious.

_____

_____

_____

2 How would you ensure that a worker's attention was drawn to information about costs?

_____

_____

_____

3 Why is it important to thank a member of the workteam for suggestions on reducing costs?

_____

_____

4 Why is it useful to use a checklist when examining your work area for ways to decrease costs?

_____

_____

Answers to these questions can be found on page 72.

4 Summary

■ To make the workteam cost conscious:

  ■ involve them;
  ■ pass on information;
  ■ give them feedback.

■ Information about costs needs to be:

  ■ in simple terms which we can relate to;
  ■ available where and when the costs are incurred.

Performance checks

Write down your answers in the spaces below to the following questions on *Controlling Costs*.

Question 1   Complete the equation: Sales − Costs = _____

Question 2   What is meant by fixed costs?

_____

Question 3   With what are holding and reorder costs associated?

_____

Question 4   How would you define the wages of security staff in cost terms?

_____

Question 5   Why cannot a first line manager always control costs?

_____

Question 6   Name two types of standard.

_____

Question 7   Why are variances analysed?

_____

Question 8   What is indicated by an adverse efficiency variance?

_____

Question 9   Name the two elements of standard cost.

_____

Question 10   What is a cost centre?

_____

Question 11   Briefly explain how a cost code is used.

_____

_____

_____

Question 12   Briefly explain what is meant by idle time.

_____

Question 13   Why are service centre costs transferred to product centres?

_____

_____

Question 14   Why is it important to get the workteam fully involved in controlling costs?

_____

_____

Question 15   How can you maintain the interest of your workteam in controlling costs?

_____

_____

Answers to these questions can be found on page 73–4.

2   Workbook assessment

Read the following case incident and then deal with the questions which follow, writing your answers on a separate sheet of paper.

■   Pat is the catering supervisor of an organization which has decided to provide lunch for its 300 employees.

Senior managers have estimated that 80 per cent of their employees will use the restaurant for a meal on five days a week for 50 weeks in a year.

The menu, with limited choice, will be offered at a self-service counter.

An average meal is not to exceed 90p in cost to the restaurant.

The following estimates have been made.

■   Gas, electricity and heating: £8000.
■   Crockery, cutlery and replacements: £1500.
■   Cleaning, laundry and sundries: £2500.

Pat, as catering supervisor, is paid £10,000 a year.

Wages for kitchen and other staff are £440 a week for 52 weeks in a year.

1 How many meals will Pat need to provide daily?

2 What is your estimate for the number of meals per year?

3 Identify and quantify the following costs for a cost statement.

   a Labour costs.
   b Material costs.
   c Overheads.
   d Sales required to cover the costs.
   e The average selling price per meal needed to cover costs.

4 If the organization decides to charge £1 for a three-course lunch, how much is it going to have to subsidize each meal?

5 What percentage will this organizational subsidy be of the annual sales through the restaurant?

6 As catering supervisor Pat has many areas of the restaurant and kitchen to control. What are they? Explain as fully as you can what Pat will need to control and how.

Portfolio of evidence B1.1, B1.2

3 Work-based assignment

60 mins

The time guide for this assignment gives you an approximate idea of how long it is likely to take you to write up your findings. You will need to spend some additional time gathering information, perhaps talking to colleagues and thinking about the assignment. As you research and report, you should aim to develop your personal competency too in focusing clearly on results and influencing others with the aim of improving cost control. Ensure that you talk to people at mutually acceptable times so that the information you receive is of the best quality and that people are fully committed to helping you. You may need to convince them of the value of your work, for instance.

This Activity may provide the basis of evidence for your S/NVQ portfolio. If you are intending to take this course of action, it might be better to write your answers on separate sheets of paper.

There may be some form of cost control in your workplace. The following questions ask you to find out something about it and your role in the cost control system.

Take any product or service which your workplace is involved with and discover the following.

1   The cost of the product or service. If it is a service, explain the cost in the form of an appropriate cost unit.

2   The prime cost of the product – this is all the direct costs.

3   The overheads content of the product/service cost broken down into:

a   factory or production overheads;
b   administrative overheads;
c   selling and distribution overheads.

4   The cost centre that you are connected to and the total cost of that cost centre for the year broken down where appropriate into departments and overheads.

5   The way in which the importance of cost control is communicated and how the workforce is motivated towards cost awareness. What is your role in this?

If this is not possible, use the checklists for keeping costs down to provide data for a report to your manager or trainer.

Prepare a report entitled 'Improving our control over costs' after analysing the effectiveness and relevance of present systems. Make appropriate recommendations for improvements and discuss your findings with your manager or trainer.

Reflect and review

1 Reflect and review

Now that you'll have completed your work on *Controlling Costs*, let's review our workbook objectives.

You should be better able to:

■ understand the types of costs and the way standard costs are determined.

You have seen direct and indirect costs, reorder and stock-out costs associated with stock. And you also looked at a number of overheads.

■ Which types of cost are under your control? What flexibility do you have in controlling them?

_____

_____

_____

_____

Fixed and variable costs are also important in organizations. It is unlikely that you can do much about fixed costs but you can make best use of resources under your control which may be measured as variable costs.

■ Can you identify anything you can do to improve the way you manage resources under your control?

_____

_____

_____

Some organizations use standard costing which can be determined as ideal, expected or current standards. If used in your organization, do you feel that they are determined and used in the best way to motivate your workteam?

■ Make a note of improvements you could recommend or put into action.

_____

_____

_____

_____

■ Identify the main areas of cost.

Costs can be classified in order to analyse them in the workplace. This allows us to record and control costs. We have worked through costing and in doing so seen how costs occur. Everything that happens within the workplace leads to a cost in some way.

■ As a first line manager, can you clearly identify the main areas of cost in your work area and are you aware of the types of cost? Do any areas need clarifying? Make notes of any points which come to mind below.

_____

_____

_____

_____

■ Is your role in controlling costs clear, bearing in mind some areas of cost may need clarification? Are you fully in control of costs which are your responsibility? Are clarifications or changes needed?

_____

_____

_____

■ Understand how to arrive at target costs for control.

Target costs are used as a standard against which to measure our performance. Standard costing is a common way of arriving at variances from target, allowing first line managers to make adjustments and take action to keep costs down.

■ Do you feel that all target costs identified in your work area are appropriate? Should you recommend to your manager that the targets should be altered, even if you found that standards were determined in a logical way? Why? Make a note of any changes you could propose.

_____

_____

_____

_____

■ Do you receive information about variances in a timely way? Would earlier receipt of information improve your effectiveness and how could this be achieved?

_____

_____

_____

_____

■ Describe cost centres and the allocation of costs.

To plan for the future, maintain control and measure performance we need detailed cost information. A good way of doing this is to allocate costs into cost centres against locations such as:

■ departments;
■ groups of machines;
■ individuals.

For cost centres to operate properly, first line managers need to record and communicate accurate information about the hours worked, idle time, material costs and so on.

■ Can you think of ways to improve communication in your workplace? Make a note of any suggestions you have for change below.

_____

_____

_____

■ Do you feel costs are appropriately allocated at present? Suggest changes for a fairer allocation below.

_____

_____

_____

■ Maintain cost consciousness.

Maintaining a good cost control system takes effort and can be frustrating, especially when you are working hard to keep the costs down but still finding it difficult to keep within budget. Controlling costs is a test of leadership. You will need to be aware of cost overruns, be able to communicate problems to management and your workteam, and involve your workteam in keeping costs down.

■ How do you communicate the importance of controlling costs? Do you use notices and change them regularly so they are not ignored? Do you talk directly to your workteam about cost control? Make a note of any improvements you feel you can make.

_____

_____

_____

_____

_____

■ Is cost control rewarded in your workplace? Should it be? Perhaps you have some thoughts you can write down now to discuss with your manager in the future.

_____

_____

_____

_____

2 Action plan

Use this plan to further develop for yourself a course of action you want to take. Make a note in the left-hand column of the issues or problems you want to tackle, and then decide what you intend to do, and make a note in Column 2.

The resources you need might include time, materials, information or money. You may need to negotiate for some of them, but they could be something easily acquired, like half an hour of somebody's time, or a chapter of a book. Put whatever you need in Column 3. No plan means anything without a timescale, so put a realistic target completion date in Column 4.

Finally, describe the outcome you want to achieve as a result of this plan, whether it is for your own benefit or advancement, or a more efficient way of doing things.

Desired outcomes	1 Issues	2 Action	3 Resources	4 Target completion	Actual outcomes

3 Extensions

Extension 1	Book	*Financial Control for Non-Financial Managers*
	Author	David Irwin
	Edition	First edition, 1995
	Publisher	Pitman

Extension 2	Book	*Controlling Costs*
	Author	John F. Gittus
	Edition	First edition, 1992
	Publisher	Kogan Page

Extension 3	Book	*Drury's Management and Cost Accounting Spreadsheet Applications Manual*
	Author	Alicia M. Gazeley
	Edition	Third edition, 1995
	Publisher	Chapman & Hall

Extension 4	Book	*Cost Control: A Strategic Guide*
	Author	David Doyle
	Edition	First edition, 1994
	Publisher	Kogan Page

These extensions can be taken up via your NEBS Management Centre. They will either have them or will arrange that you have access to them. However, it may be more convenient to check out the materials with your personnel or training people at work – they may well give you access. There are good reasons for approaching your own people; for example, they will become aware of your interest and you can involve them in your development.

4 Answers to self-assessment questions

Self-assessment 1 on page 15

1 Direct materials costs can be allocated directly and in total to an item being produced whereas indirect materials costs have a more general use in an organization and cannot be allocated directly and in total.

2 As reporters have a regular wage and advertising staff receive commission:

- the wages of the advertising staff are VARIABLE COSTS;
- the wages of the reporters are FIXED COSTS.

3 a Direct labour cost CAN be TOTALLY allocated to a particular product.
  b Wages which CANNOT be allocated to a particular product are INDIRECT labour costs.
  c Direct labour costs are often VARIABLE costs because they increase or decrease in proportion to the production being carried out.

4 The wastage of components used in the production of hard disks should be under Sam's control. Sam is not likely to be involved in marketing and sales so advertising is not controllable by Sam, nor is Sam's basic salary which would be set by senior managers.

Self-assessment 2 on page 26

1 (a) A standard cost is a PREDETERMINED cost which is achieved by setting STANDARDS related to particular circumstances or conditions of work.

2 The two reasons for setting performance standards are:

- to measure actual performance;
- as a basis for costs.

3 The standard cost of a vase is £2.50, calculated as follows:

Standard cost sheet
Direct materials: £8.00 ÷ 4 = £2.00
Direct wages: £5.00 ÷ 10   = £0.50
£2.50

4 Direct material cost variances comprise a usage variance and a price variance. Direct labour cost variances comprise an efficiency variance, an idle time variance and a rate variance.

5 A favourable variance indicates that actual costs are less than standard costs. An adverse variance indicates that actual costs are greater than standard costs.

71

Self-assessment 3 on page 48

1 a The components of prime cost are direct materials and direct labour.
  b Factory overheads are added to prime cost to arrive at the total factory cost.

2 A cost centre is a location where costs can be identified, grouped together and then finally related to a cost unit.

3 A good cost system enables costs to be:

■ collected:
■ analysed;
■ controlled.

4 The two main functions of the costing department as far as labour costs are concerned are:

■ to maintain job cost sheets for each job;
■ to analyse total wages between various cost centres.

5 Allocation is taking an overhead which belongs entirely to one cost centre completely to the costs of that cost centre. Overheads which are spread over a number of cost centres are controlled by one cost centre and the costs are then apportioned or shared out over other cost centres.

Self-assessment 4 on page 60

1 The three keys to success are:

■ Involvement;
■ Communication;
■ Feedback.

2 Workers should be provided with information in a form they can relate to and at a time and place where the cost is incurred.

3 It is important to give feedback to encourage further cost-consciousness and to motivate workers to implement cost-cutting measures.

4 A checklist helps to channel thoughts and avoids the possibility of overlooking matters.

5 Answers to activities

Activity 16 on page 21

Here are my completed calculations to compare with yours.

Standard cost sheet	
Direct materials: 5 metres at £6.10	£30.50
Direct wages:	
Moulder 1½ hours × £4.00	£ 6.00
Cutter 2½ hours × £5.00	£12.50
	£49.00

So the standard cost of a table is £49.

**Activity 24
on page 37**

Obviously, since some of our codes provide a group of numbers, your suggested cost codes may not be exactly the same as mine but I hope you can see how cost codes are actually made up.

Here are the numbers I would use:

- Theatre 1 staff nurse's salary: 098 026
- Theatre 2 medical equipment: 099 400 or any number to 449
- Physiotherapy department medical equipment: 264 400 to 449
- Drug coded 459 and ordered for the pharmacy: 171 459
- Canteen cook's wages: 400 197

**Activity 27
on page 41**

I hope we can agree on the following figures:

Regular time 40 hours at £6.00	240.00
Overtime premium 3 hours at £9.00	27.00
Gross earnings	£267.00

**Activity 35
on page 47**

£15,000 will be transferred from maintenance to Department A and £3000 to Department B.

6 Answers to the quick quiz

Answer 1 Sales – Costs = profit

Answer 2 Fixed costs are costs incurred whether anything is being produced or not.

Answer 3 Stock.

Answer 4 As an indirect labour cost or overhead.

Answer 5 Some costs are incurred by the organization as a whole.

Answer 6 Ideal, expected or current standards.

Answer 7 To aid control and planning.

Answer 8 The workteam spent longer making the product than the standard indicated.

Answer 9 Costs and performance levels.

Answer 10 A location into which direct costs and overheads are gathered.

Answer 11   A cost code identifies particular types of cost and assists in analysis of the extent of these costs used in particular centres and throughout the organization.

Answer 12   Idle time is unproductive time – not spent on actual production.

Answer 13   Because ultimately all costs must be charged against production.

Answer 14   Costs can only be controlled if the workteam is committed.

Answer 15   Through communication and feedback.

7 Certificate

Completion of this certificate by an authorized person shows that you have worked through all the parts of this workbook and satisfactorily completed the assessments. The certificate provides a record of what you have done that may be used for exemptions or as evidence of prior learning against other nationally certificated qualifications.

Pergamon Open Learning and NEBS Management are always keen to refine and improve their products. One of the key sources of information to help this process are people who have just used the product. If you have any information or views, good or bad, please pass these on.

NEBS
MANAGEMENT
DEVELOPMENT

SUPER SERIES

THIRD EDITION

Controlling Costs

....

has satisfactorily completed this workbook

Name of signatory ....

Position ....

Signature ....

Date ....

Official stamp

SUPER SERIES

SUPER SERIES 3

0-7506-3362-X   Full Set of Workbooks, User Guide and Support Guide

A. Managing Activities

0-7506-3295-X	1. Planning and Controlling Work
0-7506-3296-8	2. Understanding Quality
0-7506-3297-6	3. Achieving Quality
0-7506-3298-4	4. Caring for the Customer
0-7506-3299-2	5. Marketing and Selling
0-7506-3300-X	6. Managing a Safe Environment
0-7506-3301-8	7. Managing Lawfully - Health, Safety and Environment
0-7506-37064	8. Preventing Accidents
0-7506-3302-6	9. Leading Change

B. Managing Resources

0-7506-3303-4	1. Controlling Physical Resources
0-7506-3304-2	2. Improving Efficiency
0-7506-3305-0	3. Understanding Finance
0-7506-3306-9	4. Working with Budgets
0-7506-3307-7	5. Controlling Costs
0-7506-3308-5	6. Making a Financial Case

C. Managing People

0-7506-3309-3	1. How Organisations Work
0-7506-3310-7	2. Managing with Authority
0-7506-3311-5	3. Leading Your Team
0-7506-3312-3	4. Delegating Effectively
0-7506-3313-1	5. Working in Teams
0-7506-3314-X	6. Motivating People
0-7506-3315-8	7. Securing the Right People
0-7506-3316-6	8. Appraising Performance
0-7506-3317-4	9. Planning Training and Development
0-75063318-2	10. Delivering Training
0-7506-3320-4	11. Managing Lawfully - People and Employment
0-7506-3321-2	12. Commitment to Equality
0-7506-3322-0	13. Becoming More Effective
0-7506-3323-9	14. Managing Tough Times
0-7506-3324-7	15. Managing Time

D. Managing Information

0-7506-3325-5	1. Collecting Information
0-7506-3326-3	2. Storing and Retrieving Information
0-7506-3327-1	3. Information in Management
0-7506-3328-X	4. Communication in Management
0-7506-3329-8	5. Listening and Speaking
0-7506-3330-1	6. Communicating in Groups
0-7506-3331-X	7. Writing Effectively
0-7506-3332-8	8. Project and Report Writing
0-7506-3333-6	9. Making and Taking Decisions
0-7506-3334-4	10. Solving Problems

SUPER SERIES 3 USER GUIDE + SUPPORT GUIDE

0-7506-37056	1. User Guide
0-7506-37048	2. Support Guide

SUPER SERIES 3 CASSETTE TITLES

0-7506-3707-2	1. Complete Cassette Pack
0-7506-3711-0	2. Reaching Decisions
0-7506-3712-9	3. Managing the Bottom Line
0-7506-3710-2	4. Customers Count
0-7506-3709-9	5. Being the Best
0-7506-3708-0	6. Working Together

To Order - phone us direct for prices and availability details
(please quote ISBNs when ordering)
College orders: 01865 314333 • Account holders: 01865 314301
Individual purchases: 01865 314627 (please have credit card details ready)

We Need Your Views

We really need your views in order to make the Super Series 3 (SS3) an even better learning tool for you. Please take time out to complete and return this questionnaire to Sarah Scott-Taylor, Pergamon Open Learning, Linacre House, Jordan Hill, Oxford, OX2 8DP.

Name :...

Address :...

....

Title of workbook :...

If applicable, please state which qualification you are studying for. If not, please describe what study you are undertaking, and with which organisation or college:

....

Please grade the following out of 10 (10 being extremely good, 0 being extremely poor):

Content   ....   Appropriateness to your position   ....

Readability   ....   Qualification coverage   ....

What did you particularly like about this workbook?

....
....
....

Are there any features you disliked about this workbook? Please identify them.

....
....
....

Are there any errors we have missed? If so, please state page number: ....

How are you using the material? For example, as an open learning course, as a reference resource, as a training resource etc.

....

How did you hear about Super Series 3?:

Word of mouth: ☐   Through my tutor/trainer: ☐   Mailshot: ☐

Other (please give details):...

....

Many thanks for your help in returning this form.

Pergamon Flexible Learning *for tomorrow's managers*
T OF BUTTERWORTH-HEINEMANN

&₊NEBS Management

der your workbooks just tick the box beside your selection.

Complete set of workbooks and CD-ROM	07506 52969	£900.00
	+ VAT on CD:	£55.13
Complete set of workbooks	07506 3362X	£650.00
Super Series 3e CD	07506 52381	£350.00
	+ VAT:	£61.25
Leading Your Team	07506 33115	£18.99
Working in Teams	07506 33131	£18.99
Motivating People	07506 3314X	£18.99
How Organisations Work	07506 33093	£18.99
Delegating Effectively	07506 33123	£18.99
Delivering Training	07506 33182	£18.99
Planning Training and Development	07506 33174	£18.99
Managing Time	07506 33247	£18.99
Managing Tough Times	07506 33239	£18.99
Managing with Authority	07506 33107	£18.99
Managing Lawfully – People and Employment	07506 33204	£18.99
Appraising Performance	07506 33166	£18.99
Commitment to Equality	07506 33212	£18.99
Securing the Right People	07506 33158	£18.99
Becoming more Effective	07506 33220	£18.99
Communicating in Groups	07506 33301	£18.99
Communication in Management	07506 3328X	£18.99
Project and Report Writing	07506 33328	£18.99
Listening and Speaking	07506 33298	£18.99
Writing Effectively	07506 3331X	£18.99
Making and Taking Decisions	07506 33336	£18.99
Solving Problems	07506 33344	£18.99
Information in Management	07506 33271	£18.99
Storing and Retrieving Information	07506 33263	£18.99
Collecting Information	07506 33255	£18.99
Leading Change	07506 33026	£18.99
Understanding Quality	07506 32968	£18.99
Achieving Quality	07506 32976	£18.99
Planning and Controlling Work	07506 3295X	£18.99
Auditing Quality	07506 4091X	£18.99
Caring for the Customer	07506 32984	£18.99
Marketing and Selling	07506 32992	£18.99
Managing A Safe Environment	07506 3300X	£18.99
Managing Lawfully – Health, Safety and Environment	07506 33018	£18.99
Preventing Accidents	07506 37064	£18.99
Managing Energy Efficiency	07506 40928	£18.99
Controlling Physical Resources	07506 33034	£18.99
Controlling Costs	07506 33077	£18.99
Understanding Finance	07506 33050	£18.99
Making a Financial Case	07506 33085	£18.99
Improving Efficiency	07506 33042	£18.99
Working with Budgets	07506 33069	£18.99
User Guide	07506 37056	£18.99
Support Guide	07506 37048	£18.99
Audio Cassettes – The complete set of 5	07506 37072	£49.99

Total cost of selection(s) £

Total VAT (if selections include CD) £

Please add £3.00 for UK and European surface post delivery: £
(Please add £6.00 for air mail delivery)

ORDER TOTAL

UTTERWORTH-HEINEMANN PAPERBACKS

tterworth-Heinemann publish a wide range of books that are complimentary Super Series 3. To find out more, visit: www.bh.com/management

HOW TO ORDER

BY MAIL Please complete this order form and return to: Vicki Cottrell, Pergamon Flexible Learning, Linacre House, Jordan Hill, Oxford, OX2 8DP.

BY PHONE Call our CUSTOMER HOTLINE on 01865 888190
Quoting Ref: B102BHDL01

BY FAX Fax this order form to Customer Services on 01865 314290

BY EMAIL bhuk.orders@bhein.rel.co.uk

Please attach this order form to an official purchase order (only for orders in the UK over £100).

Remittance enclosed £

Cheques should be made payable to: Heinemann Publishers Oxford.

See full details of all our products and register for Pergamon's free e-mail update service for Training Managers by visiting: www.bh.com/pergamonfl

Name (please print)

Company name

Job title

Address

Postcode   Country

Telephone   Fax

Email address

Date

METHOD OF PAYMENT

Please debit my credit card as follows: Access   Barclaycard/Visa
Amex   American Express   Diners Club   Switch
Card number

Expiry Date: /   Signature:

PERGAMON FLEXIBLE LEARNING BUTTERWORTH-HEINEMANN GUARANTEE
We are confident that you will be fully satisfied with any book that you order from us. However, if you are not totally happy then you can return the book in a saleable condition with the invoice within 30 days and receive a full refund.

Please arrange for me to be kept informed of other books, journals and information services on this and related subjects. This information is being collected on behalf of Reed Elsevier plc and may be used to supply information about products produced by companies within the Reed Elsevier plc group.

Orders are normally dispatched within 5 days of receipt of the order, however, if the book(s) are not available within 28 days your money will be refunded. Where books are not yet published, they will normally be dispatched within 5 days of publication. All publication dates, prices and other details are correct at time of going to press but may be subject to change without further notice.

Reed Educational & Professional Publishing Ltd, Registered Office: 25 Victoria Street, London SW1 0EX Registered in England Number 3099304. VAT No: 663 347230.

For more information or to discuss your training needs, please contact one of our Key Account Managers:

David Lockley (North of England and Scotland)
Tel: 01772 715273   E-mail: david.lockley@repp.co.uk
or
Chris Brooks (Ireland, Wales and the South of England)
Tel: 01993 852026   E-mail: christopher.brooks@repp.co.uk

Or contact your local distributor. You can find their details at: www.bh.com/pergamonfl